Praying
for your
Husband

CHAYIL PRAYER JOURNAL

mildred kingsley-okonkwo

Published and Printed in Nigeria by:

MillionValues Concepts,
105, Igi-Olugbin, Pedro Road, Lagos
Tel: 08185710897 | millionvalues@gmail.com

To contact the author:

Tel: 08077714411, 08077714413

Kingsley,

..for always making me believe …in God…in love …in you

Thank You

Kingsley Okonkwo- the wind beneath my wings. You propel me. You make me better. You cheer me on and you celebrate my victories. No one will ever convince me that God doesn't love me...see the man He gave me. I love you forever and a day. You make loving you and praying for you so easy.

Hadasaah, Davida and David for all the times I said "I'm sorry, Mummy is busy" and you didn't hold it against me. For being so young and understanding that I don't belong to only you but to as many as Jesus has sent me to.

Family is everything. My parents Mr and Mrs Chijide and my parents' in-law HRH and Ugoeze Okonkwo. My love and endless gratitude.

My ladder holders on this project- Kemi, Blessing and Femi-for working with me on crazy deadlines.

For making my life easier- Mabel, Amaka, Diche and Happiness.

To all those who call me mama especially Eziaha-for

always praying and expecting so much that I am forced to be more and do more.

My pastor Rev Albert Femi Oduwole for always always making me believe...Thank you sir. I definitely aim to make you very proud.

The amazing Chayil women at David's Christian Centre. You inspire me to be a better wife every day.

...to my dear reader

It is definitely an honor and a privilege to share with you some of the scriptures I have prayed over my husband in the last couple of years that we have been husband and wife.

I understand how hard it can be to be an effective wife and mother and one of the ways to ensure that it doesn't become harder is to ensure that the one you are called to help is in line with the plan God has for both of you. It would be a disaster to be married to someone who just doesn't get it; there's nothing as bad as being under a terrible or confused leader. However, we must come to terms with the fact that a great husband is not born he is made. So, your prayers will go a long way into making him the kind of husband he should be.

So, your husband is not Mister perfect? Thankfully, you can do something about it — you can pray! No, you cannot complain about him, nag or become difficult because it will change nothing. But you can change things some other way. How? You can pray! And you should pray which is why I am putting this book in your hands.

Seeing as I am not married to your husband though, I may not have the specifics but I can share with you the scriptures I have used. They can be a guide for you to build your own prayer pattern for your husband. I also threw in some action points, things to think about and questions that can help you talk more to your husband or guide you into knowing the specifics to pray about.

Please note this is not necessarily a method cast in stone. It is a prayer suggestion and since they have worked tremendously for me, I share them in confidence that they will work for you too because the word of God never fails and God is not partial. What He does for one, He does for all.

Here's to testimonies…

With all my love,
Pastor M.

Action: print and paste a picture of your husband.

This is _____ *the Love of my
life, the king of my heart, the gift of God to me. I make
a commitment to pray for him every day till he becomes all
that God has destined for him to be.*

One

When Boaz Comes

Now there was a wealthy and influential man in Bethlehem named Boaz…
—Ruth 2:1a (NLT)

One of the greatest revelations I have ever had concerning marriage has been this: marriage is not a reward; it is an assignment. We are not married because we are more special than the single girl out there, it is because God has a job for us to do. We are on a mission. I truly believe that God sends us into the lives of our husbands to help them be the very best versions of themselves. No matter how great a man is, he can be greater.

I also think that the Proverbs 31 Chayil woman was everything she was because she had the kind of man that let her. He was a man also fulfilling his own destiny – living out his purpose. He was respected and influential; he was described as a major voice in the nation since it tells us he sat at the city gates among the elders of the land, probably making policies. One of our major assignments is to make sure that our husbands emerge as Boaz – prosperous and well respected. These are the two major needs every man has - to be successful and to be influential.

Prayer: Lord, I pray that _____will achieve his full potential. He will be wealthy, prosperous, successful, influential and well respected. He will be a voice in this nation and generation in Jesus name.

Further Meditation: Proverbs 31:23

Let's take a little walk… back to when you fell in love with your husband. The moment you knew he was the man you wanted to spend the rest of your life with; that he was your Boaz.

Five reasons why you chose him

1. ....
2. ....
3. ....
4. ....
5. ....

Five things that define success and being influential for your husband

1. ....
2. ....
3. ....
4. ....
5. ....

Marriage is not a reward;
it is an assignment.

Journal

Two

The Cost of Anger

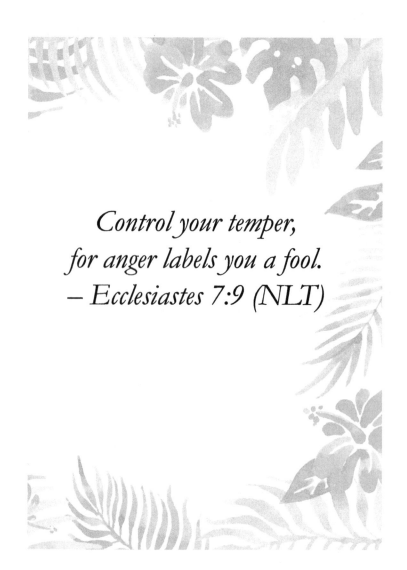

*Control your temper,
for anger labels you a fool.
— Ecclesiastes 7:9 (NLT)*

An angry man is dangerous. A hot-tempered man makes very poor decisions that can destroy not only himself but all those around him. I have seen women end up dead just because their husbands were not able to control their tempers. A hot-tempered man is very difficult to discuss with. He can be very irrational and unreasonable. An angry man will not listen even when what is being said to him makes sense. Because Moses acted in anger, he missed out on entering the Promised Land; that's what anger will do to you.

Uncontrolled anger can destroy all that one has worked hard for in just few minutes. Men have lost their jobs, reputations and even families because of uncontrolled anger. You do not want your husband to pay the cost of anger. It's much too high.

Prayer: Lord, I ask that you will teach _____ to control his temper and keep his cool at all times. No matter the provocation, he will not lose his temper or sin, make mistakes or take foolish actions. I declare the fruit of the Spirit is at work in his life making him walk in patience and understanding and helping him direct his energies wisely in Jesus name.

Further Meditation: Numbers 20:6 -12, Proverbs 14:9, Proverbs 29:22.

What are the things that annoy my husband the most?

1. ....

2. ....

3. ....

4. ....

5. ....

How do I react when my husband is upset?

....

....

Is there a better approach to take?

....

....

Something to think about:
- In marriage anger is a wasted emotion. Never go to bed angry, always solve the issue or forget about it and move on.
- Always practice advance forgiveness, even when he doesn't apologize. So that your prayers for him will not be hindered.
- Always remember you don't quench fire with fire.
- Always remember a soft answer turns away wrath.

Journal

Three

Money Magnet

If you start thinking to yourselves, "I did all this. And all by myself. I'm rich. It's all mine!" — Well, think again. Remember that God, your God, gave you the strength to produce all this wealth…
-Deuteronomy 8:17-18a (MSG)

oney is a major necessity in marriage. Correct me if I'm wrong but I don't believe that any marriage can be truly happy without the basic necessities of life. As much as I would like to tell you that love is all you need to sustain a marriage; that would be a lie. Love doesn't pay school fees, the house rent or medical bills. I also need to stress that one of the areas the enemy attacks men the most is in their finances.

No matter how anointed a man is, if he is struggling financially, he will be frustrated and in turn frustrate you. So you need to pray that there will be a free flow of finances in his life; that he will make, multiply and manage money well. The only way to ensure this is that he constantly sees God as his source.

Prayer: Dear God, I recognize that you are the one who gives _____ the power to get wealth. Help him never forget that. Help him to make, manage and multiply our finances through the wisdom that you give him. I thank you because all our bills are paid and all our needs are met. I declare that he prospers in every currency and is a money magnet in Jesus' name.

Further Meditation: Philippians 4:19

Something to think about

- Money is very important in marriage but it must never be the foundation of your marriage.

- Money is a tool. It is meant to be used not worshipped.

- Never fight over money; Money lost can always be made but hurtful words are hard to make right.

- Never let money destroy the bond of trust you have for each other if it is becoming a problem find creative ways to work around it.

- Let faith be the determining factor not money when making critical decisions in your marriage.

List the areas your husband needs money the most

1. ....

2. ....

3. ....

4. ....

5. ....

No matter how anointed a man is,
if he is struggling financially, he will be frustrated.

Journal

Four

Above all things

Beloved, I wish above all things that you may prosper and be in health, even as your soul prospers - 3 John 1:2 (NKJV)

*H*aven't you ever wondered why being in health is paramount on God's list of desires for us? Well, I have and I have come to the conclusion that no matt er how rich, how talented or happily married you are all it takes to really mess it all up is to have failing health. Paying medical bills, even if it is a curable disease, can take its toll on anyone. Also having a spouse who is always sick can squeeze the life out of any marriage. No one wants to be neck-high in hospital bills or always caring for a sick spouse.

Thankfully, we have a healer and even better, a God who can actually keep us from being sick. Don't accept any form of sickness in your husband's life, even headaches. It's not a part of the covenant. Expect him to be a whole man – spirit, soul and body.

Prayer: I pray that _____will constantly walk in divine health. I declare that by every stripe Jesus took on the cross his body is exempt from sickness and disease. I declare that sickness has no place in his body. Because the spirit of God dwells inside him, his body rejects any form of sickness or disease. He remains strong and healthy for as long as he lives in Jesus name.

What is your husband doing that is a risk factor to his health?

1. ....

2. ....

3. ....

4. ....

5. ....

How can you help your husband live a healthier life this year?

1. ....

2. ....

3. ....

4. ....

5. ....

Something to think about

- The only way to achieve all you are called to do is in a healthy body. A sick body is limiting.

- Being healthy isn't only limited to eating clean, exercising and drinking lots of water it is also having a healthy mind.

- Keep the space in your husband's life peaceful. Peace brings health.

Journal

Five

Faith Not Fear

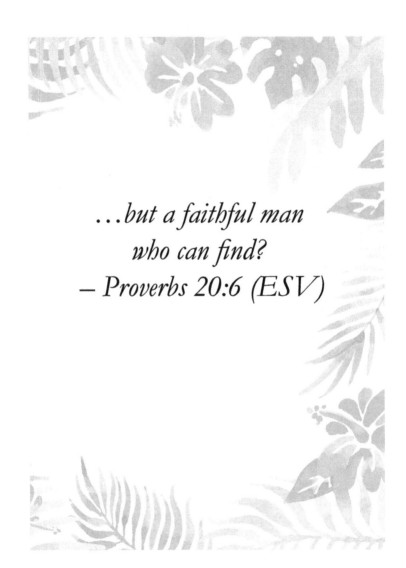

*...but a faithful man
who can find?
– Proverbs 20:6 (ESV)*

know this scripture is talking about a man who is faithful, steadfast and loyal but this scripture often speaks to me in a different way. I usually interpret it as a FAITH FULL man. In other words, a man who is full of faith, a man who will respond to whatever life throws at him with faith. No woman wants a coward for a husband; you need someone who you know will stand boldly and declare deliverance where necessary, one who will make faith moves when it's time to change gears in your lives.

Funny enough, contrary to what we think, a lot of men are prone to fear on a daily basis. They have moments when their hearts can fail and they begin to battle with uncertainty. The things that God will ask your husband to do and the dreams that God will give him that will change your lives will always be bigger than his mind can contain. They would usually require faith and a lot of courage. So pray that his heart would be strengthened and faith would rise in his heart till you can say that he is a faith FULL man; a man FULL of faith.

Prayer: Father, I pray for _____ that he will always be very strong and courageous. I pray that he will never respond to challenges with fear but he will be a man full of faith and move in the power of the Holy Spirit at all times in Jesus name.

Further Meditation: Joshua 1:9

Which areas do you think he needs to exhibit more faith?

1. ....
2. ....
3. ....
4. ....
5. ....

Name memorable testimonies born out of your husband's faith. Share them with him. These testimonies will remind both of you of how faith can totally alter your lives and if he has never believed God for anything, this would be a good time to start.

1. ....
2. ....
3. ....
4. ....
5. ....

When fear knocks on the door, let faith answer

Journal

Six

Better Here

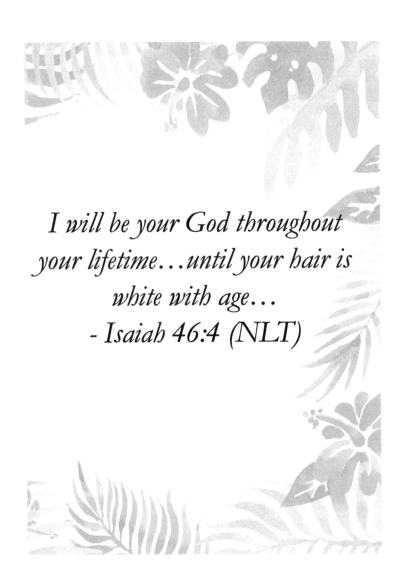

I will be your God throughout your lifetime…until your hair is white with age…
- Isaiah 46:4 (NLT)

friend of mine recently lost her husband. As I sat with her, I noticed she had aged instantly with grief. As she sat there with tears freely flowing down her face and intermittent palpitations wracking through her body, it hit me that no matter how annoying your spouse sometimes gets, you never wish him dead. He's always better with you… *here*.

The journey of life is always better with someone beside you; someone who will be a father to your children and a spiritual, emotional and sometimes financial cover to you. When you are hit with the cold stormy moments of life knowing that you are not alone matters. As I sat there, and people came and went, I thought to myself "She will go into that empty room – no live-in lover, no friend, no brother or partner. She's all alone." The longer I have my husband here on earth with me the better.

Prayer: I pray that _____ is here with me till all his hair turns grey. I pray that he will live till he is satisfied and he can say like Paul I have finished my course and I have run my race. _____ will live a long, healthy and fulfilled life in Jesus name.

Further Meditation: Psalm 91:16

Two people are better than one,
because they get more done by working together [a good return for
their hard work/toil].
If one falls down, the other can help him [his colleague] up. But it
is bad [a pity] for the person who is alone and falls,
because no one is there to help.
– Ecclesiastes 4: 9-10 Expanded Bible (EXB)

I'm thankful .... Is here with me because

1. ....
2. ....
3. ....
4. ....
5. ....

*At the end of the day, life is better when
you're doing it with someone else*

Journal

Seven

Renewed Life

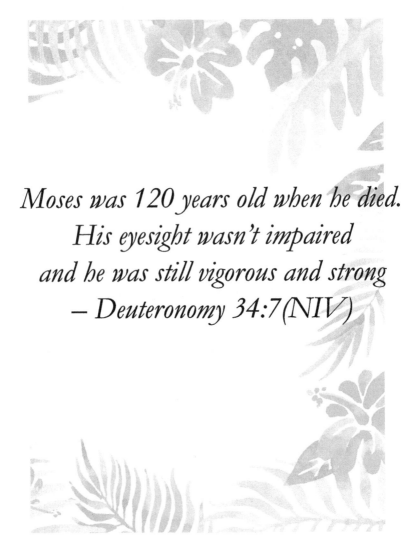

*Moses was 120 years old when he died.
His eyesight wasn't impaired
and he was still vigorous and strong
— Deuteronomy 34:7 (NIV)*

*R*ecently I was talking to a well-respected medical doctor and she was lamenting on how, in Nigeria, there is presently inadequate care for the elderly and no proper healthcare plan for them. They are pretty much left to die – with a lot of age-induced illnesses.

However, the Bible makes it clear that long life is not the only thing covered in the covenant. We are expected to age well too. Moses was 120 years yet his eyesight did not get dim. I've heard a lot of people say that your eyesight gets worse with age. Well, not in the covenant. The Bible says that Moses' body was not enveloped in aches and pains but he was still vigorous and strong.

Pray that even as your husband gets older, he will still be like Caleb conquering mountains and doing great things irrespective of his age.

Prayer: I pray for _____ he will not be a liability in old age. _____ will be strong and healthy. He will age well – his eyesight will be perfect, his strength will be renewed, his mind will be alert. He will still be as relevant and active as he was as the husband of my youth. Like fine wine, as he gets older, he will get better in Jesus name.

Further Meditation: Joshua 14:10-11

The eagle has the longest life-span of its species. It can live up to 70 years. But to reach this age, the eagle must make a hard decision. In its 40's its long and flexible talons can no longer grab prey which serves as food. Its long and sharp beak becomes bent. Its old-aged and heavy wings, due to their thick feathers, become stuck to its chest and make it difficult to fly. Then, the eagle is left with only two options: die or go through a painful process of change which lasts 150 days. The process requires that the eagle fly to a mountaintop and sit on its nest. There the eagle knocks its beak against a rock until it plucks it out. After plucking it out, the eagle will wait for a new beak to grow back and then it will pluck out its talons. When its new talons grow back, the eagle starts plucking its old-aged feathers. And after five months, the eagle takes its famous flight of rebirth and lives for 30 more years.

who satisfies your desires with good things so that your youth is renewed like the eagle's. – Psalm 103:5 (NIV)

I saw this excerpt online and totally loved the analogy because everyone has to do certain things while they still can to ensure that they age well. I think also praying so your husband knows what to shed so he can live a productive life and age well is so important.

Journal

Eight

Angels On Guard

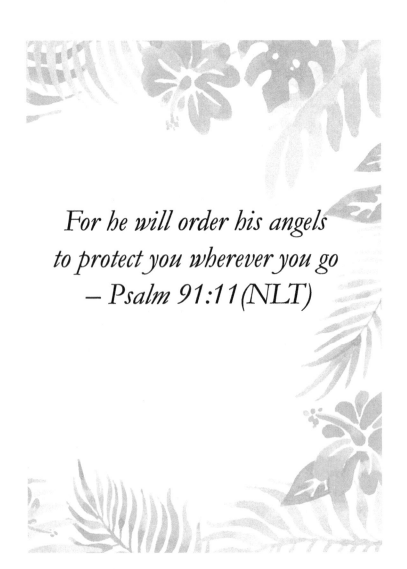

*For he will order his angels
to protect you wherever you go
– Psalm 91:11(NLT)*

s I write this, my husband is not in town. He's been away for three weeks and the truth is, the only reason I sleep well at night (as well as I can possibly sleep in an empty bed) is because I know that even though I can't watch him constantly, God's angels can. My trust is in God to keep him safe at all times. Praying for his protection is non-negotiable because the enemy is prowling looking for whom he may devour but the Bible tells us that as far as we dwell in the secret place of the Most-High and abide under the shadow of the Almighty, that we are protected under God's wings. Protected from accidents, sickness, armed robbers and thieves, bad friends, deceivers, reputation killers – just name it.

Prayer: Lord, I pray that your angels will guard _____ constantly. He will remain under your wings at all times protected from every evil. I pray that no matter what comes his way, he will constantly be conscious of your hand of protection over him. I declare that _____ will never be caught in an accident, he will be kept safe from armed robbers, deceivers and any form of destruction in Jesus name.

Further Meditation: Psalm 23:4; Psalm 91:3-4

Personally, I have had many angelic encounters. I believe in angels and I believe they are everywhere around me. I still remember very vividly one night the year I got married, my husband and I went out to get some ice cream. On our way home, I saw something that caught my eye and even though my husband was driving I called his attention to it. In that split second that he took his eyes off the road, he didn't see a big hole right in the middle of the road. It was too late to swerve, we practically jumped in and out of it then we heard a very loud bang, then a hiss and our tyre went flat.

This was about 1:30am, on a very dark and lonely road with no help in sight. We checked the booth of the car thankfully there was a spare and a jack but we also discovered that we needed a special wrench which we didn't have. After we had been waiting a while with no cars passing by, suddenly, a car drove past, stopped, and parked a few feet away from us. A man wearing a white "danshiki" got out, walked to the car asked what the problem was, went to his car and brought the exact wrench we needed. He also went ahead to change the tyre all by himself. Once he was done, he said good night, got into his car and left. What are the odds?

Obviously, an angel sent by God to rescue us.

Angels are around us, you just need to open your eyes to see them.

Journal

Nine

When He Is Thirsty

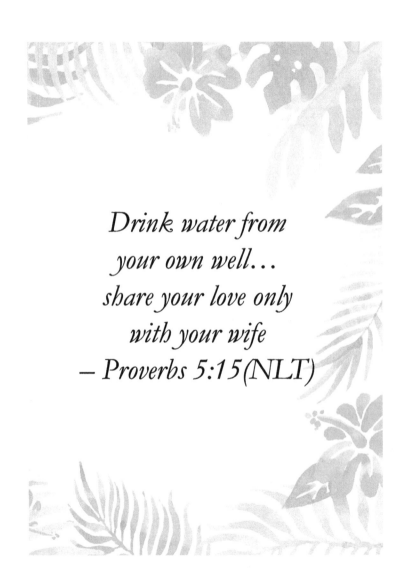

Drink water from
your own well…
share your love only
with your wife
— Proverbs 5:15 (NLT)

Have you ever been really, really thirsty? Like almost dying of thirst, throat parched, tongue stuck to the roof of your mouth kind of thirst? Now if the only thing around you is diesel would you drink it? I'm guessing not. So why is it okay for husbands to do that? Too many husbands are either drinking polluted water or another man's water (stolen waters). What do I mean by that? **ADULTERY!!!**

Adultery is dangerous to a man's life and marriage. First, it destroys the covenant with his partner, eliminates trust between them and leaves him open to the ravages of sin and sickness. It opens him up to satan and his attacks. God's desire is that the covenant of marriage will be strengthened through sex in marriage. Pray that your husband drinks water from your well alone.

Prayer: I pray that _____ will drink waters from my own well. He will never be caught in acts of adultery. I declare that he will find pleasure in me at all times and never be drawn into any other woman's arms. Every other woman will be sexually repulsive to him in Jesus name.

Further Meditation: Proverbs 5:20

Honor marriage, and guard the sacredness of sexual intimacy between wife and husband. God draws a firm line between casual and illicit sex - **Hebrews 13:4 (MSG)**

Sexual drives are strong, but marriage is strong enough to contain them and provide for a balanced and fulfilling sexual life in a world of sexual disorder. The marriage bed must be a place of mutuality-the husband seeking to satisfy his wife, the wife seeking to satisfy her husband. Marriage is not place to "stand up for your right." marriage is a decision to serve the other, whether in bed or out.
-1Corinthians 7:2-4 (MSG)

Ask yourself?

- What am I doing to keep myself sexually attractive to my husband?
- How often do I have sex with my husband in a month?
- How often do I turn him down and why?
- When was the last time we had sex? Who initiated?
- Is your husband sexually lazy? What can you do to help?
- Are there creative ways to make our sex lives better?

Something to think about:
When a man has a large meal and is full, he has no space to snack. **(In Nigerian lingo – Man wey don chop pounded yam for house no dey buy gala for road).**

Journal

Ten

Dead Meat

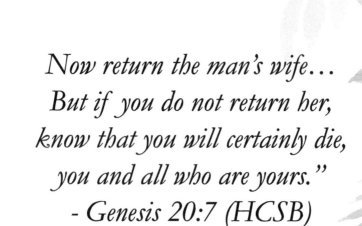

Now return the man's wife…
But if you do not return her,
know that you will certainly die,
you and all who are yours."
- Genesis 20:7 (HCSB)

*F*or a long time, I didn't really think much of this scripture until recently. At least I never saw it in the light that I have in the last weeks. One of the things we must learn to do is fight where we have strength. As Christian wives we can't fight dirty so what do we do? We fight where we can – on our knees.

Abraham couldn't face king Abimelech but God could and that's what a covenant partner does, he fights for you. God sent a death threat to Abimelech and I can hear him send one to that girl who won't let your marriage be. "Release her husband or you are dead meat!!!" So, you can simply rest in this that God is fighting for you and you fight on your knees. Break the hold the enemy has on your husband (if any) in the place of prayer.

You can also send forth a threat in the spirit to dissuade the enemy from having any plans on your husband or marriage.

Prayer: Father I thank you that _____ is set free from the clutches of any and every strange woman. I invoke my covenant rights with you and I declare that you fight for me. Anyone who tampers with or threatens my marriage is already dead to him. No mountain can survive before me she is made plain ground and my husband only has eyes for me in Jesus name.

Further Meditation: Proverbs 7:5-27.

Abraham moved south to the Negev and lived for a while between Kadesh and Shur, and then he moved on to Gerar. While living there as a foreigner, Abraham introduced his wife, Sarah, by saying, "She is my sister." So King Abimelech of Gerar sent for Sarah and had her brought to him at his palace.

But that night God came to Abimelech in a dream and told him, "You are a dead man, for that woman you have taken is already married!" But Abimelech had not slept with her yet, so he said, "Lord, will you destroy an innocent nation? Didn't Abraham tell me, 'She is my sister'? And she herself said, 'Yes, he is my brother.' I acted in complete innocence! My hands are clean."

In the dream God responded, "Yes, I know you are innocent. That's why I kept you from sinning against me, and why I did not let you touch her. Now return the woman to her husband, and he will pray for you, for he is a prophet. Then you will live. But if you don't return her to him, you can be sure that you and all your people will die." – **Genesis 20: 1-7**

Just harboring another man's wife in his house almost got Abimelech killed how much more someone sleeping with your spouse. You have every right to fight back in the place of prayer.

Journal

Eleven

The Best Pathway

The LORD says, 'I will guide you along the best pathway for your life. I will advise you and watch over you.
– Psalm 32:8 (NLT)

*E*veryone has a pathway for their life. God created us with our own particular lanes in destiny. True success is getting to your destination via your own ordained pathway. God promises to, not only show us the pathway but to guide us along the best pathway for our lives. The truth is as they say in this part of the world, "There are many roads that lead to the market" but you want your husband to know which pathway is his and which is the best path for him to take. That way, he saves time and energy and gets the maximum result possible.

Too many men struggle to know their paths but God is so amazing because He doesn't just show us the best path, He is also advising us while we are on it and He promises to watch over us to make sure we get it right on that path. So why let your husband struggle when God has offered to help?

Prayer: Father, I pray that _____ will have continuous guidance from you. He will know the best pathway for his life. I pray that his ears will constantly hear your advice. He will never be stranded because he will always have divine direction in Jesus name.

Further Meditation: Isaiah 30:21

She had always loved writing but never thought of it as anything more than a hobby. Being a doctor, she applied for her residency programme but didn't get in. A lot of her friends got in and though she was happy for them, she felt bad not just because it was the next step in her career but because she felt left behind.

Two years later she applied again. The date for the entrance exam was postponed several times and eventually clashed with an important family engagement. She somehow missed the exam. She was confused and depressed- this was supposed to be easy. There was a path for doctors to take and it seemed like she was missing it. She prayed; God's response was simple; Jeremiah 29:11.

God ordered her steps into the movie industry as a writer. In such a short time and with very little formal training, she has worked on projects that have aired on the most prominent TV stations and worked with the industry's finest producers and directors. Not to mention the very good pay and flexible schedules.

This is a testimony I have been privy to personally. Even though she thought her pathway to success was medicine and taking her exams, God knew her pathway to success and He helped her find it. If you pray your husband will not miss his pathway to success even when it is not obvious or it doesn't make sense.

True success is getting to your destination via your own ordained pathway.

Journal

Twelve

Just Hanging Out

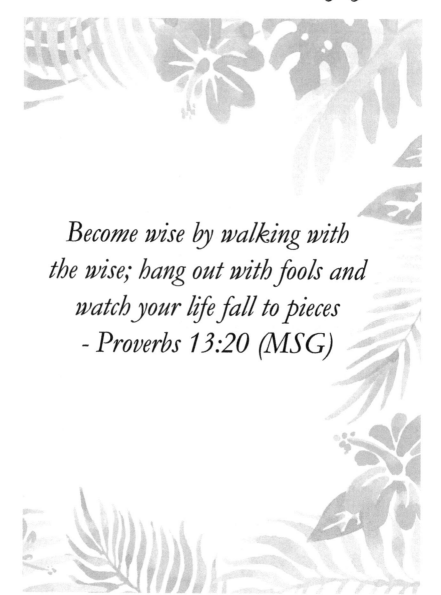

Become wise by walking with the wise; hang out with fools and watch your life fall to pieces
- Proverbs 13:20 (MSG)

*I*f you have ever heard these words: "We are just hanging out", then you may understand why this is such an important thing to pray about. Your husband's friends play a major role in his life. They influence his thoughts and eventually his actions. The people that he calls friends are a reflection of the kind of person he can be and the kind of ideas he will be open to accepting.

I still remember reading the story of Tamar in (**2Samuel 13:1-2**) who was raped by her half-brother Amnon. Incidentally, Amnon was just sulking and not planning to do anything about the feelings he was experiencing because he was decent enough to respect the fact that she was a virgin. Everything was fine till verse 3, where the Bible says "…but Amnon had a **FRIEND** whose name was Jonadab." Everything went downhill from there and eventually led to Amnon's death. Whom your husband hangs out with matters a whole lot, it can determine the outcome of his life.

Prayer: Lord, I pray that you will surround _____ with godly friends. He will not follow evil advice, he will not hangout with friends who belittle the things of God. He will only have friends that love You and delight in doing what You want them to do in Jesus name. His friendships will be productive and not distract him from the things of God in Jesus name.

Further Meditation: Psalm 1:1

My husband's close friends are?

1. ....
2. ....
3. ....
4. ....
5. ....

Qualities I want to see in his best friends?

1. ....
2. ....
3. ....
4. ....
5. ....

Never underestimate the power of friendship.

Once you identify your husband's closest friends and you identify the qualities you want in them if not already in existence, you start praying for them to be. Praying for your husband's friends is not optional it's a necessity.

*Show me your friends and
I will show you your future…*

Journal

Thirteen

A Way Of Escape

And no temptation is irresistible. You can trust God to keep the temptation from becoming so strong that you can't stand up against it…He will show you how to escape…
1 Corinthians 10:3 (TLB)

A Way Of Escape

The Bible makes it clear that temptation is common to man. There's no human being who does not encounter temptation. As long as you are human, you will encounter some form of temptation. Even the Bible tells us that Jesus was led into the wilderness to be tempted by satan. Now the interesting thing is that even though he was tempted with the same things all men are tempted with – "...**the lust of the flesh, the lust of the eyes and the pride of life" (1 John 2:16),** Jesus always had one answer "GET THEE BEHIND ME SATAN!" He could see right through the temptation, and he always had a way of escape.

Don't delude yourself that your husband doesn't get tempted to lie, cheat, steal or commit adultery because he does. What you should do is pray that he sees it for what it is and recognizes the way of escape that the Lord has promised.

Prayer: Lord, I thank you that _____ is under your watchful eyes and because you were a man and fully understand what it means to be tempted you will help him to constantly see the way of escape from every temptation without sinning in Jesus name.

Further Meditation: Hebrews 4:15; Matthew 4:1-11.

She kept putting pressure on Joseph day after day, but he refused to sleep with her, and he kept out of her way as much as possible. One day, however, no one else was around when he went in to do his work. She came and grabbed him by his cloak, demanding, "Come on, sleep with me!" Joseph tore himself away, but he left his cloak in her hand as he ran from the house.
-Genesis 39:10-13(NLT).

Three things that your husband battles with the most?

1. ....

2. ....

3. ....

4. ....

5. ....

Journal

Fourteen

Who Is Guiding You?

And I will give you shepherds after my own heart, who will guide you with knowledge and understanding.
– Jeremiah 3:15 (NLT)

Who Is Guiding You?

*T*he person speaking into your husband's life is so important because to a large extent, he influences the outcome of your life and marriage. And the truth is there is little you can do in choosing them because if you are not careful, you can come across as being disrespectful or domineering. However, you can pray that he will pick the right pastors, mentors and bosses in his life; that he will have people who give him godly counsel and model a godly lifestyle for him. If his mentors are adulterous wife-beaters, chances are he would be too. So, your best bet is to influence this decision in the place of prayer.

Prayer: I pray that you will give _____ leaders, pastors and mentors that will always give him good and godly counsel, people that will guide him to make the right decisions concerning our lives and marriage. I pray that they will model a life patterned strictly after the word of God in Jesus name

Further Meditation: 2 Samuel 16:23

Who is your husband most accountable to?
What is their relationship?
Who does he go to for counsel?
Does he fully obey the counsel he receives?

Who are the biggest influences in your husband's life?

1. ....

2. ....

3. ....

4. ....

5. ....

List 1 quality you desire he will pick from each of them

1. ....

2. ....

3. ....

4. ....

5. ....

*A Mentor is the picture of your future
so choose wisely*

Journal

Fifteen

The Heart Of The Matter

After removing Saul, he made David their king. God testified concerning him: 'I have found David son of Jesse, a man after my own heart; he will do everything I want him to do.'
– Acts 13:22 (NIV)

*T*he same way appliances are remote-controlled, human beings are also controlled. However, the only difference is that man is heart controlled not remote controlled. So the state of a man's heart largely determines the outcome of his life. The Bible tells us to guard our hearts with all diligence because from it all the issues of life are determined.

You need to pray that he will be a man who God holds the remote to his heart and life. A man whose heart is focused on God and pleasing him, a man whose heart yearns for God constantly and desires to please Him alone, will easily make you a very happy wife because he will only do what God wants him to do and once God finds a man like that, his elevation is inevitable.

Prayer: I pray that _____ will be a man after God's heart, a man that will obey God quickly and at all times. His heart will consistently long for God the same way the deer pants for water. I declare that _____ has a heart that is tender towards the things of God and receptive to His word in Jesus name.

Further Meditation: Proverbs 4:23, Psalm 51:10

Something to think about

A good man brings good things out of the good stored up in his heart, and an evil man brings evil things out of the evil stored up in his heart. For the mouth speaks what the heart is full of
– Luke 6:45 (NIV)

For as he thinketh in his heart, so is he:
-Proverbs 23:7a (KJV)

But the LORD said to Samuel, "Don't judge by his appearance or height, for I have rejected him. The LORD doesn't see things the way you see them. People judge by outward appearance, but the LORD looks at the heart."
– 1 Samuel 16:7 (NLT)

So, just thinking about these scriptures shows me that God looks beyond a man's actions right into his heart. That's where the real connection happens between God and a man. So it is important that you pray that his heart remains in the right place so he can stay connected with God and hear God clearly. God speaks better to a man who he knows will obey him.

Journal

Sixteen

Where Are The Fathers?

"Yes, I've settled on him as the one to train his children and future family to observe God's way of life, live kindly and generously and fairly, so that God can complete in Abraham what he promised him."
- Genesis 18:19(MSG)

*T*he Bible is very clear on parenting expectations. God's desire is that the children learn to love Him from their fathers; that fathers are exemplary in their relationship with God especially because children learn more from what they see than what they are told.

Every husband should be like Abraham. God should be able to vouch for the fact that he will teach his children to follow God's ways. Unfortunately, no one is born a father. No one comes with the blueprint, so you need to pray for your husband to be the kind of father that will ensure your children fulfill destiny just by emulating him.

Prayer: I pray that _____ will direct our children to keep the way of the LORD by doing what is right and just, so that the LORD will bring about for _____ what He has promised him. I pray that He will not be like Eli afraid to correct and discipline our children instead he will be a strong spiritual mentor to them in Jesus name.

Further Meditation: 1 Samuel 3:10-14.

Where Are The Fathers?

Ask yourself

What is your husband's relationship with his father like?

What kind of childhood did he have? Was he close with his father?

What kind of father is your husband? Is he a hands-on or absentee father?

Is he fulfilling his role of fatherhood with your children? What more would you like him to do?

What can you do to re-inforce it?

Is he a spiritual role model for your children?

Have you often felt the need to take over his role and be both father and mother?

Has that made you a bit resentful?

The answers to these questions will help you pray for your husband not to make the same parenting mistakes his father made (if any) and to pray practical steps into his life for a better relationship with your children so they can begin to see him as a role model which is ultimately God's plan.

Journal

Seventeen

Opportunity Cost

"I will give you hidden treasures, riches stored in secret places…"
–Isaiah 45:3(NIV)

Opportunity Cost

*T*here are two things that will always come our way –challenges and opportunities. You don't necessarily need to pray for them. You do however have to pray to be able to recognize them because the cost of missing an opportunity can be truly devastating and can slow down progress in life.

One of the ways to be great in life is to see what others are not seeing. The man who sees opportunities before they are apparent to others will always be the leader. For your husband to stand out among his peers, he needs to recognize the opportunities that God will bring his way. God says there are hidden treasures; these treasures are not hidden from him, they are hidden for him. There are riches stored in secret places and God gladly reveals secrets to his children if we will only ask.

Prayer: I pray that every opportunity that God has hidden for _____ his eyes will be open to see them and he will have the boldness and courage to follow through on them. _____ will not miss his God-ordained opportunities. He will see them early enough, recognize them and have the strength to follow through on them in Jesus name.

Further Meditation: Jeremiah 33:3

Marco Polo is one of the most famed explorers of history. It seems he inherited the travel bug from his father. In 1260, when Marco polo was 6, his father and uncle traveled to Mongolia (part of modern-day China). When they arrived there the Mongol emperor revealed an interest in Christianity. He asked the brothers to take a letter to the Pope requesting as many as 100 wise men to spread the Gospel among his subjects.

Three years later the brothers arrived home, and two years later set out on their return trek. Did they take the 100 wise men with them? No. Just two friars, for this was all the church felt they could spare. And even those two didn't make it, turning back shortly into their journey.

What a tragedy! Imagine if the Kublai's request had been fulfilled. Perhaps the whole history of China may have been changed.

Reference: National Geographic, May 2001.

This story keeps turning in my heart. Just imagine if that "small" opportunity" was taken, who knows China may have been a Christian nation today. It's so crucial our husbands don't take opportunities for granted no matter how unimportant they may seem at the time they arise.

Journal

Eighteen

What Time Is It?

He changes times and
seasons; he removes kings
and sets up kings…
– Daniel 2:21 (AMP)

*E*very time I read about the people who did great things in the Bible, I notice something very peculiar. Sometimes, it wasn't even that they were special; it just was their time and season. Sometimes they had been doing the same thing consistently and one day an opportunity came calling and they were promoted from prison to palace. David had been in the bush, unknown, keeping the sheep. Then one day, when it was his time, Goliath was brought down with the same shepherd's sling he had probably used to kill lizards, a bear and a lion.

Jesus understood how important time was. He told his mother "My hour has not yet come." It's important that we don't jump ahead of time but that we also don't miss our time. Now God has the power to make it your husband's time so don't you think that should be something you should sort out in the place of prayer? Time and opportunity create promotion. Let's call it forth.

Prayer: Lord, I know that you are the one who changes times and seasons and promotes men into kingship. I declare that this is the time and season for _____ to enter the fullness of his kingship in life and to fulfill his destiny and he will recognize and understand it. I declare that he will not miss the right timing in Jesus name.

Further Meditation: 1 Chronicles 12:32

Something to meditate on:

Everything has its own time, and there is a specific
time for every activity under heaven:

a time to be born and a time to die, a time to plant
and a time to pull out what was planted,

a time to kill and a time to heal, a time to tear down
and a time to build up,

a time to cry and a time to laugh, a time to mourn
and a time to dance,

a time to scatter stones and a time to gather them, a
time to hug and a time to stop hugging,

a time to start looking and a time to stop looking, a
time to keep and a time to throw away,

a time to tear apart and a time to sew together, a
time to keep quiet and a time to speak out,

a time to love and a time to hate, a time for war and
a time for peace.
Ecclesiastes 3:1-8(GWT)

Journal

Nineteen

Let Him Ask

If any of you needs wisdom to know what you should do, you should ask God, and he will give it to you. God is generous to everyone and doesn't find fault with them.
— James 1:5 (GWT)

s a husband and the head of the home, your husband will need to make a lot of decisions and that will require constantly knowing what to do and when he should do it. If you ask me, he's going to need large doses of wisdom because the decisions he will take will affect you and your children and possibly generations after him. There's one way to ensure that he makes the right decisions: you pray! Yes, pray!

The Bible says if anyone needs wisdom, and we know that leaders definitely need wisdom, let him ask God. Praying for wisdom for him will be more productive than nagging him or worse still, ignoring him with a 'that's his business, when he messes up, he will learn' attitude. That way may be too costly to gain experience. It is better he gets it right from the start by operating with God's wisdom.

Prayer: Dear Lord, thank You for making provision for wisdom and thank You that it will be freely given to _____ without criticizing or faultfinding. I pray that like Solomon, wiser than all the wise men from the east and the wise men from Egypt (the world). His wisdom will clearly be from God in Jesus name.

Further Meditation: 1 Kings 4:30

That night the Lord appeared to Solomon in a dream, and God said, "What do you want? Ask, and I will give it to you!" Solomon replied, "You showed great and faithful love to your servant my father, David, because he was honest and true and faithful to you. And you have continued to show this great and faithful love to him today by giving him a son to sit on his throne.

"Now, O Lord my God, you have made me king instead of my father, David, but I am like a little child who doesn't know his way around. And here I am in the midst of your own chosen people, a nation so great and numerous they cannot be counted! Give me an understanding heart so that I can govern your people well and know the difference between right and wrong. For who by himself is able to govern this great people of yours?"

The Lord was pleased that Solomon had asked for wisdom. So God replied, "Because you have asked for wisdom in governing my people with justice and have not asked for a long life or wealth or the death of your enemies— I will give you what you asked for! I will give you a wise and understanding heart such as no one else has had or ever will have! And I will also give you what you did not ask for—riches and fame! No other king in all the world will be compared to you for the rest of your life!"– **1 kings 3:5-13 (NLT)**

Journal

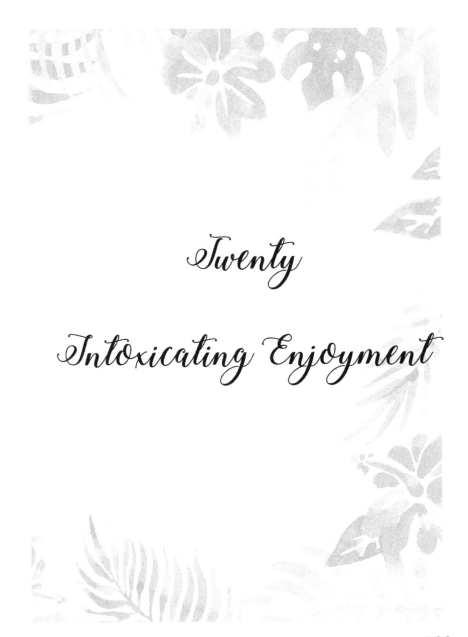

Twenty

Intoxicating Enjoyment

Let your own fountain be blessed, and enjoy the girl you married when you were young, a loving doe and a graceful deer. Always let her breasts satisfy you. Always be intoxicated with her love.
— Proverbs 5:18-19(GWT)

*M*arriage is to be ENJOYED not ENDURED. Anything people enjoy, they stick to. Have you ever wondered why people get addicted to things? They start out enjoying those things then it progresses to addiction. They can't seem to do without that particular substance. If your husband enjoys being with you and gets satisfaction from his marriage, he is likely to spend more time working on your marriage and whether we like it or not marriage is work. It requires attention and commitment. So pray that he finds everything he needs in you.

In the scripture it states that your breasts will satisfy him at all times. Your breasts are a symbol of provision and sustenance. That means you will have what he needs and he will keep coming back for more till he's intoxicated by you. You will provide help and satisfaction for him and he will be sustained in your marriage.

Prayer: I pray that my marriage with _____ **is blessed. I pray that he will enjoy our marriage, he will not endure it. My breast will satisfy him always till he is intoxicated by me. He will not need anyone else. Our sex life and marriage will keep getting better every year in Jesus name.**

Further Meditation: 1 Corinthians 1:1-7.

Ask yourself

Would you consider your husband your friend?

Would you say that you are as close or closer than before you got married?

What did you enjoy doing with your husband when you were dating?

1. ....

2. ....

3. ....

4. ....

5. ....

What things would you say have become a distraction?

1. ....

2. ....

3. ....

4. ....

5. ....

*A lasting marriage requires hard work
but few tasks reap a finer reward.*

Journal

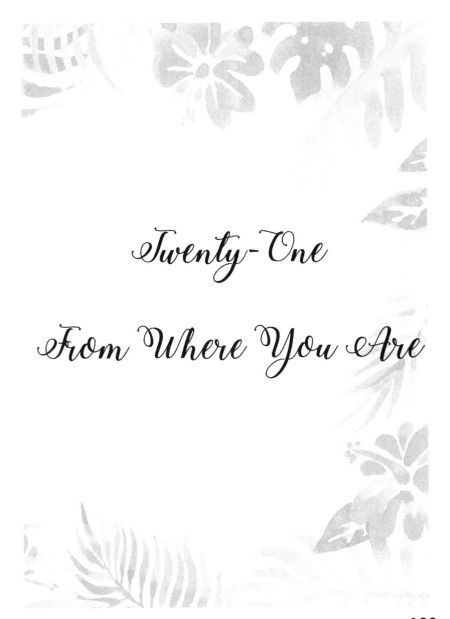

Twenty-One

From Where You Are

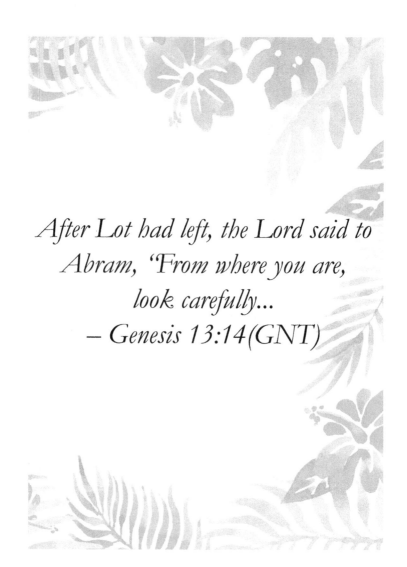

After Lot had left, the Lord said to Abram, "From where you are, look carefully...
— Genesis 13:14(GNT)

I believe this prayer is in two parts and I think it's important that we don't miss it.

First, I believe that Lot being in Abraham's life was holding him back from hearing the instruction for the next level. So, we need to get rid of every Lot that is keeping your husband from hearing God. Lot doesn't necessarily have to be a person. It's just anything or anyone that wants to keep you in your comfort zone.

So after Lot left, then God spoke clearly and what He said was "from where you are, look CAREFULLY…" This tells me the key to his next level may be staring your husband in the face where he is now but until he can actually look carefully to see, he will remain where he is. Pray that he will see and recognize his next level.

Prayer: I declare that every Lot in _____ life will leave; everything keeping him from hearing God clearly for the next level will be removed from his life. I pray that he will have seeing eyes and hearing ears, that he will recognize opportunities before him and not belittle them. I pray that he will know when to make a move for his next level in Jesus name.

Further Meditation: Proverbs 20:12.

Something to think about:

Your big opportunity may be right where you are now-
Napoleon hill

When you see yourself as a powerful creator of your conditions, you'll see opportunities to get to your goals and dreams - all around you
Robin S. Sharma

When people walk away from you let them go, your destiny is never tied to people who leave you. It doesn't mean they are bad people it just means their part in your story is over
Anonymous

When the wrong people leave your life, the right things start happening
Anonymous

If you're brave enough to say goodbye, life will reward you with new hello
Paulo Coehlo

The key to your next level is always in this level
-Kingsley Okonkwo

Journal

Twenty-Two

Visible Progress

…and the rod of Aaron of the tribe of Levi had burst into bloom! It sprouted buds, bloomed blossoms, and produced fully ripe almonds!
–Numbers 17:8 (ISV)

*L*ife is never stagnant; if you are not moving forward then you are ultimately moving back. It's not enough for your husband to be doing well, he should be making progress; moving from one level to the next, seamlessly. Every day should be better than the previous. I often hear my husband say *"we have never had a better last year"* and that for me is a real blessing because it is proof that he is making progress.

The Bible tells us that Aaron's rod burst into a bloom showing that it was alive and productive but it didn't stop there. It also budded, meaning it entered another level of progress. Then it blossomed, meaning yet another level of progress. Then it produced almonds but not just almonds, fully ripe almonds showing visible and obvious fruitfulness.

Prayer: I pray that _____ will make consistent and remarkable progress in every area of his life – at work, in his spiritual life and in his family. Like Aaron's rod, his life will burst into bloom; it will bud, bloom, blossom and produce fully ripened results. Every level of his life will be from glory to glory. Every year he lives, he makes tangible, recognizable progress in Jesus name.

Further Meditation: Psalm 92:12

Visible Progress

What are the levels of progress your husband has recorded from when you got married till now?

1. ....

2. ....

3. ....

4. ....

5. ....

List the areas of visible progress you would like to see in your husband's life in the next one year.

1. ....

2. ....

3. ....

4. ....

5. ....

Writing it down will help you trace where he is making his least progress so you can pull in more spiritual resources in that area-prayer, wisdom, searching the word for answers or direction to help him make progress.

A little progress every day adds up to better results.

Journal

Twenty-Three

Secret Desires

May he give you the desire
of your heart and make all
your plans succeed
— Psalm 20:4 (NIV)

*T*here are some things that only God and your husband know how deeply he desires it, and the fact is he may never tell you about it. They are desires imbedded deeply into his heart. You may never hear about them, but they are real nonetheless. He probably has a deeper yearning for those things than the ones he speaks about.

Your job is to key into the fact that the Holy Spirit knows what they are and pray that He brings them to pass. So rather than going round the house sulking and making it about you saying: "why is he not telling me the problem? Are we supposed to have secrets from each other? Why does he think I can't handle it?" Simply find a quiet place in your home and lay it in God's hands. Let God who sees in secret answer openly. This is a good time to pray in the spirit. Praying in tongues will help ensure you are not praying amiss.

Prayer: Father, I know you see the innermost parts of the heart so I know you know the secret desires that _____has. I pray that you grant him his heart's desires and that you cause every plan that he has, and he is working on to succeed in Jesus name.

Further Mediation: Psalm 37:4

Do you sometimes feel a disconnect between you and your husband?

Do you sometimes feel like there's more he would like to share with you but he seems to be holding back?

What are the areas you would appreciate more openness from your husband?

1. ....
2. ....
3. ....
4. ....
5. ....

What are your husband's desires you are already aware of?

1. ....
2. ....
3. ....
4. ....
5. ....

God who sees in secret will always answer openly.

Journal

Twenty-Four

The Midas Touch

The LORD will open the heavens, the storehouse of his bounty, to send rain on your land in season and to bless all the work of your hands. You will lend to many nations but will borrow from none
—Deuteronomy 28:12 (NIV)

When God made man, the first thing He gave him was work. He put him in the garden and asked him to tend it and keep it. Then He gave him an assignment. He began naming the animals; he took responsibility for everything. So even till date, men largely get their identity from what they do. From work.

A frustrated man is one who is either not doing anything or is not being productive at what he is doing. It's important that he succeeds at all his hands finds to do and that he is successful at every venture. Once a man's work is not doing well, he is likely to be very difficult to live with and making him happy will be near impossible so inevitably you too will be frustrated.

Prayer: I pray that everything _____ **does will prosper. You will bless all the works of his hands and all his ideas, and will cause all his plans to work. I pray that all his endeavors will be successful in Jesus name.**

Further Mediation: Deuteronomy 30:9

In details can you describe what your husband does as work? Give a detailed job description

....
....
....
....
....

What new ideas/vision (work-related) has your husband spoken to you about?

....
....
....
....
....

Does your husband like what he does presently?
What would he rather be doing?
Would he like to change his job?
Does he have a dream job?

At the working man's house,
hunger looks in but dares not enter
−Benjamin franklin

Journal

Twenty-Five

Not An Accident

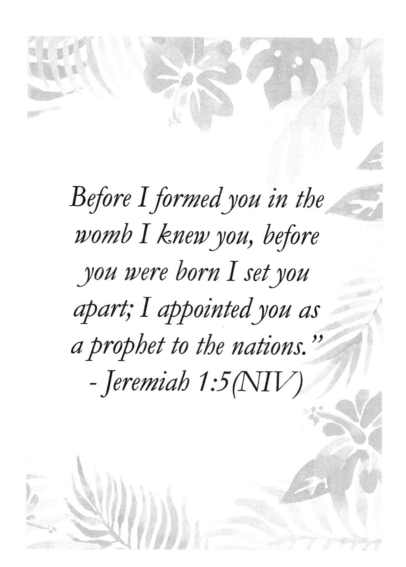

Before I formed you in the
womb I knew you, before
you were born I set you
apart; I appointed you as
a prophet to the nations."
- Jeremiah 1:5 (NIV)

*B*efore your husband was born, God knew him. It's amazing that God planned that he would be born, and he planned a specific assignment for him. I was watching a clip the other day about a man who went to heaven and the angel kept calling him evangelist. He kept saying I'm not an evangelist, I'm an accountant. I worked at so-and-so accounting firm. The angel kept saying "Evangelist, where are the 366,287 souls you were supposed to bring into the kingdom?" It got me thinking to myself how terrible it would be to live such a wasted life. How can one miss the mark so badly?

Everyone has a definite assignment. That's what you are created for in the first place. Your job is to pray your husband lives his ordained life… You better pray he does. A fulfilled man living right in the middle of his pre-ordained destiny is an amazing husband; I should know.

Prayer: Lord, I pray that _____ discovers what he was born for and fulfils the assignment God sent him to the world for. I pray that he fulfills his destiny. _____ will be a vessel in God's hand. He will not miss the mark in Jesus name.

Further Meditation: Psalm 139:13

What visions did your husband tell you about before you got married?

1. ....

2. ....

3. ....

4. ....

5. ....

Can you say he is fulfilling them?

....

What are you husband's goals and dreams for the year?

1. ....

2. ....

3. ....

4. ....

5. ....

What is your husband's life goal?

....

The purpose of life is a life of purpose

Journal

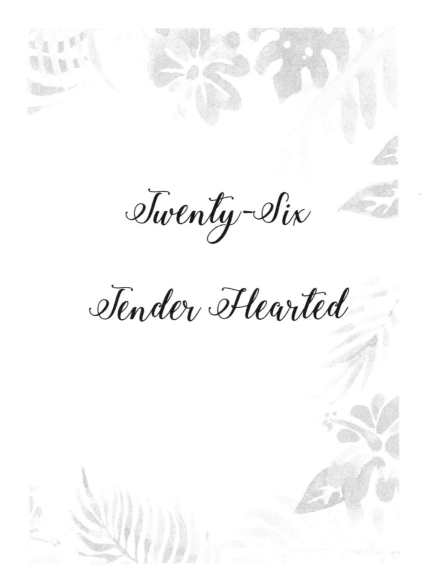

Twenty-Six

Tender Hearted

*.... I will take away their
stony, stubborn heart and
give them a tender,
responsive heart
-Ezekiel 11:19b (NLT)*

One of the things I know about my husband is that he has a heart that is responsive to God. I don't believe he got there overnight and I don't take it for granted. The thing about a heart that is tender and responsive is that once God says something, they will do it. This means that they have tenderness towards, and a love for God and His word. A man that is meek and teachable will go far in God because he will be sensitive to God and get instructions from God easily.

It's simple really. Don't you like talking to people that listen to you? I mean, really listen? Well, God is no different; if you listen, then He will speak. Your safety is tied to your husband not being a stubborn man. He needs to be tender towards the things of God. Oh! This will save you from turning into a nagging wife. This is one prayer you don't want to joke with.

Prayer: Lord, I pray that _____ will not have a stubborn stony heart. I pray that Your Spirit will be at work in him constantly and he will have a heart that is tender and responsive to You and to Your will in Jesus name.

Further Meditation: Ezekiel 36:26-27

What are the things you know your husband should be doing but he is being head strong about?

1. ....
2. ....
3. ....
4. ....
5. ....

Are there scriptures that form the foundation for you thinking your husband should do these things?

1. ....
2. ....
3. ....
4. ....
5. ....

These questions are very important to help us determine whether this is just a selfish desire in our hearts as wives or it is actually an instruction from God that is for his own good. If you don't have a scriptural backing for them then it may just be you thinking your husband needs to do this not necessarily God. So his being head strong about it may be a good thing. So you, not him may need to change.

Journal

164

Twenty-Seven

When Kings Don't Sleep

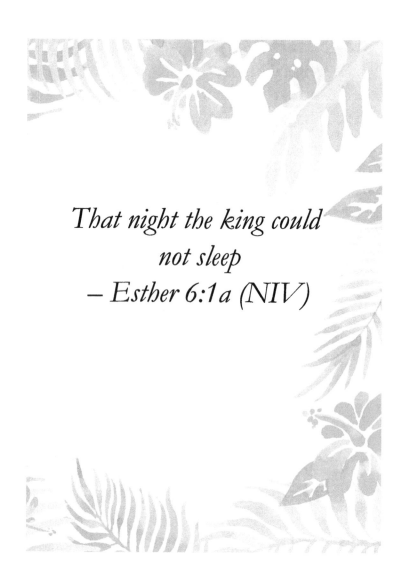

*That night the king could
not sleep
— Esther 6:1a (NIV)*

*I*n the past few years, I have learnt the importance of kings in a person's life. As my pastor who incidentally is my husband always says, **"men pay but a king rewards"**. A reward is different from regular pay. A reward covers all the years you have been paid and more. It's always much more than what you deserve. When God wants to bless you, he sends a king.

In this story, because God wanted to bless Mordecai, He gave the king a sleepless night till he asked for the book of remembrance to be brought and read to him. Then he decided to reward Mordecai for something he had even likely forgotten he did. He even used his enemy to bless him. If you ask me, that is God turning what the enemy meant for evil into good. He honored and rewarded Mordecai when he least expected it. So let's pray that Destiny helpers will remember your husband and reward him.

Prayer: Lord I pray that every king or helper of destiny that you choose to use to bless _____ will remember him. I pray that you will bring him before kings and he will not stand before mean men. I pray that every enemy of his progress will be used to favor him instead in Jesus name.

Further Meditation: Daniel 6:18

What are your husband's wildest imagination/craziest dream; the kind that even you have a hard time being in faith about?

1. ....

2. ....

3. ....

4. ....

5. ....

Are there people your husband needs to meet or has been longing to meet, that would create a turning point in his life?

1. ....

2. ....

3. ....

4. ....

5. ....

Once you identify who these people are you can pray about divine connections. However, please be careful not to put your faith in these men. God may have other plans. Keep your eyes on God. He is the Source, He can decide to change the channel He uses.

Journal

Twenty-Eight

Unhindered Prayers

...you husbands must give honor to your wives. Treat your wife with understanding as you live together. She may be weaker than you are, but she is your equal partner in God's gift of new life. Treat her as you should so your prayers will not be hindered.
— 1 Peter 3:7(NLT)

*S*ometimes when I pray this over my husband, it feels like I'm being selfish but I realize it's a ploy of the enemy to distract me. You see, if my husband treating me well wasn't so important in the equation God wouldn't have put it in the Bible. It's important that he loves and understands me so that his prayers are not hindered. Why because God is very passionate about covenant and the way he treats me shows he values covenant.

I pray for him to be more considerate of me and more compassionate toward me not just for me but for him as well. Plus, it's a foundation for my children. My daughters grow up knowing what is unacceptable from a man and they set standards for themselves while my son gets a positive role model as he learns how to treat women from his father. So you see, it's a win-win for everyone.

Prayer: Lord, because you are the all-wise God and you know all things, I pray that you will teach _____ how to love me and dwell with me with understanding so that his prayers are not hindered in Jesus name.

Further Meditation: Malachi 2:13-15

What things would you like your husband to do that are constant reminders of his love for you?

1. ....
2. ....
3. ....
4. ....
5. ....

How can you make it easier for him to love you? What are your love languages and in what order?

1. ....
2. ....
3. ....
4. ....
5. ....

What tips can you leave for him to follow?

1. ....
2. ....
3. ....
4. ....

*The best thing any man can
do for himself is to love his wife*

Journal

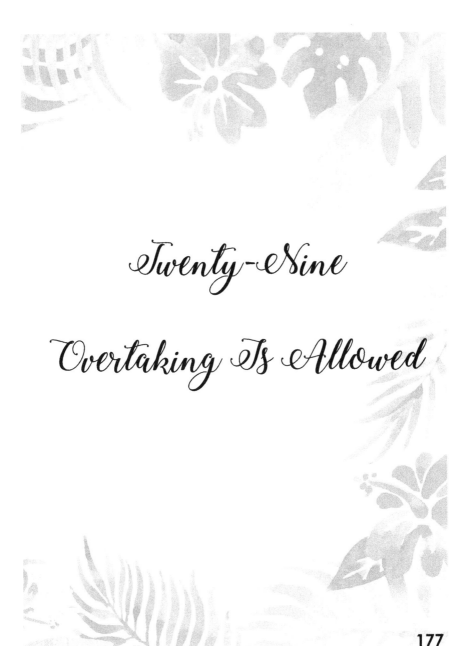

Twenty-Nine

Overtaking Is Allowed

*Then the hand of the
LORD was on Elijah, and
he girded up his loins
and outran Ahab to Jezreel.
– 1 Kings 18:46 (NASB)*

*T*his was no ordinary feat; this was a man on foot outrunning not just other men running on foot but men on horses and not just ordinary men, a king on his chariot. Everyone knows that the king's horses would be the best and fastest yet that made no difference when the hand of the Lord came upon Elijah.

This is what the hand of God on your husband's life can do. It can cause him to overtake those who are seemingly more advantaged than him. It will probably be as unexplainable as a man on foot outrunning kings on horses but when it comes to the things of God, they are not for the mind to comprehend because our God specializes in breaking protocol and doing the impossible. He wants to do the same in your husband's life.

Prayer: Father, I thank you because you are the God who specializes in miracles. I pray that your hand will be mighty upon _____ and he will overtake those who are seemingly more advantaged than him. I pray that your grace and favor will be at work in his life that doors will open to him and he will gain entrance into levels he only imagined in Jesus name.

Further Meditation: 1 Samuel 16:11

Overtaking Is Allowed

Meditate on this:

Then Jesse called Abinadab and had him pass in front of Samuel. But Samuel said," The Lord has not chosen this one either," Jesse then had Shammah pass by, but Samuel said, "Nor has the Lord chosen this one." Jesse had seven of his sons pass before Samuel, but Samuel said to him, "The Lord has not chosen these". So he asked Jesse, "Are these all the sons you have?"

"There is still the youngest," Jesse answered. "He is tending the sheep."

Samuel said, "Send for him; **we will not sit down until he arrives."**

So he sent for him and had him brought in. He was glowing with health and had a fine appearance and handsome features. Then the Lord said, "Rise and anoint him, this is the one." So Samuel took the horn of oil and anointed him in the presence of his brothers, and from that day on the Spirit of the Lord came powerfully upon David. Samuel then went to Ramah. –1Samuel 16:8-13 (NIV)

Even though David was the youngest and by right should not be considered, God still broke protocol for him. This is proof that with God overtaking is allowed.

Journal

Thirty

What Is Good

He who finds a wife finds what is good and receives favor from the LORD
– Proverbs 18:22 (NIV)

*B*eing a husband is a good thing. Anytime marriage is mentioned in the Bible, one of the words you somehow find ascribed to it is the word good. I believe that marriage has many benefits and one of the major ones is favor. Favor does a lot in a man's life. The things that labor cannot bring into your husband's life favor can and the one that favor brings is definitely better.

Favor will cause your husband to stand out. It will cause people to bless him without knowing why. It will cause him to get things he is not qualified for or deserving of. It will exempt him from consequences he deserves. Favor also protects; it is a shield around your husband and God wants to favor him RIGHT NOW so you need to pray that he is enveloped in God's favor daily.

Prayer: Lord, I thank you that the set time to favor _____ is right now. You are even more passionate about surrounding him with favor than I am. I pray that your favor will be a shield around him daily exempting him from evil consequences and causing people to bless him and help him even if they don't know him. Let favor bring to him the things he can never earn by his labor in Jesus name.

Further Meditation: Psalm 5:12; Psalm 102:13.

What Is Good

What are the areas your husband labors the most?

1. ....
2. ....
3. ....
4. ....
5. ....

What areas do you desire God to favor him?

1. ....
2. ....
3. ....
4. ....
5. ....

Praying for favor for your husband makes his life easier. And once a man has found a wife, he is entitled to favor. Use your position as a wife to call forth your husband's entitlement

186

Journal

Thirty-One

A City Without Walls

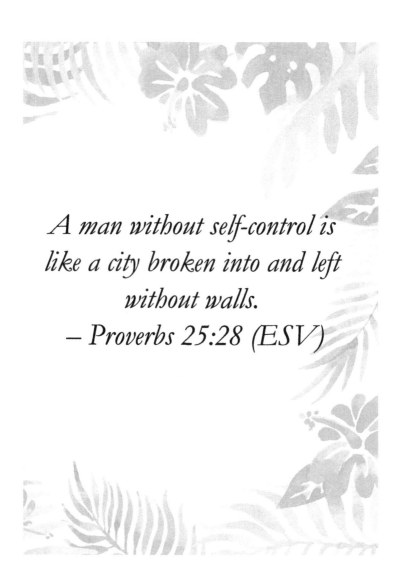

A man without self-control is like a city broken into and left without walls.
— Proverbs 25:28 (ESV)

One of the ways a man leaves himself vulnerable to the enemy's attacks is when he lacks self-control. Self-control is a major ingredient for success in life. Every man must be disciplined enough to be comfortable with using the word NO!!! It is self-control that will keep him from eating more food when he should be losing weight. It will help him say NO when he needs money and all he has left is his tithe. Self-control will keep him from putting himself in compromising situations with the opposite sex. It will keep him from saying all that is on his mind when the time isn't right. It will keep him from reacting in anger.

Self-control is delayed gratification – making sacrifices now for a better later. When a man has no self-control, he leaves himself unguarded and there is nothing as dangerous as a city without walls or a house with all its windows and doors knocked out – it is free for all to plunder.

Prayer: I declare that _____ produces all the fruit of the Spirit especially self-control. He will know when to say NO! and stick by it. I declare that his life and destiny is preserved because his life is a city with well-guarded walls in Jesus name.

Further Meditation: Titus 2:2.

What are your husband's weaknesses?

1. ....
2. ....
3. ....
4. ....
5. ....

Things would be better if he had self-control in?

1. ....
2. ....
3. ....
4. ....
5. ....

*Self-control is knowing you can
but deciding you won't.*

Put up a picture of you and your husband
(A better, happier version of both of you)

Make this journey again next month

Journal

Journal

Journal

Journal

Journal

Journal

About the Author

mildred Kingsley-Okonkwo is a Christian. A woman who firmly believes that being a woman is a calling and a ministry.

She is married to Kingsley Okonkwo her best friend and together they have taught on love, dating and marriage for over a decade. She pastors with him at David's Christian Centre.

mildred is an author who blogs at www.justusgirlsnaija.com and runs a ministry under the same name which hosts conferences bringing hope and healing to many.

She enjoys cooking, reading, pedicures, massages and long walk-not in any particular order. She and her husband are parents to three amazing miracles-'Dassah, Davida and David and make their home in Lagos, Nigeria.

Made in the USA
Middletown, DE
27 September 2023

39471623R00113